A Farmyard Christmas Pageant

Written by Donna Hert | Illustrated by Carolina Vazquez

Rover, the family dog, knew his people were getting ready for Christmas. He could hear the special music that was always played at this time of year. He could smell good things being made in the kitchen. He could see special decorations being put up everywhere, inside and outside. Things were getting very festive indeed.

Rover gave a big stretch and a little bark which told his people that he wanted to go outside. Someone opened the door for him so he could amble into the farm yard. Rover hadn't gone far before he noticed his little friend, Frances the lamb, frolicking in the meadow. He walked over to say hello. When Frances saw Rover she bounded over to the fence to greet him.

"Rover," Frances began, "you'll never guess what happened! I got the most important part in the Christmas pageant!"

"A Christmas pageant?" said Rover "You mean a play about the Christmas story?"

"Yes," said Frances excitedly, "the animals around the farm put on a Christmas pageant and this year I got the most important part!"

Now Rover knew all about the Christmas story. Sometimes when his people thought he was sleeping on the rug near the fire he was really watching, and especially listening. He had, for many years, heard his people talking about or reading the Christmas story. He heard songs that told the story and he sometimes saw his people getting ready for a Christmas pageant of their own. He knew that the story was really about love and the most important part was baby Jesus so he said, "Well, Frances, you will be a very sweet baby Jesus. That is quite the honour!"

But Frances replied, "I'm not baby Jesus!"

"I thought you said you got the most important part" began Rover, a bit confused.

"I did!" exclaimed Frances.

"Well," said Rover, "if you're not baby Jesus then you must be Mary. Because if it weren't for Mary, there wouldn't be a Christmas story. If she hadn't agreed to be the mother of Jesus I don't know what would have happened. So you're right. Mary is the most important part and you'll be fine as Mary."

"I'm not Mary." stated Frances, "Bessie the cow is Mary."

"Bessie the cow?" replied Rover curiously.

"Yeah, she's so loving and motherly, we just had to ask her to be Mary." explained Frances. "She not only gives milk to her little calf, but she lets the farmer sell her milk to people too. It's almost like she's a mother to everyone."

Rover nodded in agreement. "You know, Bessie is a good choice. Mary was the mother of baby Jesus and in a way she is mother to each of us as well. But if you're not baby Jesus and you are not Mary, then you must be Joseph! He was also very important and you would be a good Joseph. Joseph and Mary were planning to be married. They must have been so in love. Joseph knew that the baby in Mary's tummy was a special gift and he wanted to take care of Mary and the baby. Because Joseph was a carpenter, perhaps he made a nice little bed for the baby."

Frances replied, "You know, I bet Joseph was a wonderful husband and the best daddy ever. I would be honoured to be Joseph, but Paddy Beaver is Joseph 'cuz he likes to work with wood just like Joseph did."

Rover was still trying to figure out what part the little lamb played in the Christmas pageant. He looked thoughtful, put his head to one side as dogs do and said, half to himself, "OK. You're not baby Jesus. Bessie, the cow, is Mary. Paddy, the beaver, is Joseph. Now who would a little lamb be in the Christmas play?"

Frances began excitedly, "I have the most important part! I..."

But Rover interrupted, "I've got it. You are an angel! Perhaps you are the angel Gabriel who came to tell Mary that she was going to have a baby. Because, after all, if the angel hadn't come how would Mary have even known what to name the wee one? It was the angel Gabriel who told her to call the baby, Jesus."

"Nope," replied Frances, "I'm not the angel Gabriel."

Suddenly, the dog thought he knew! "OK. Then you're one of the angels that visited the shepherds to tell them that Jesus had been born! They were pretty significant. If it hadn't been for the angels how would anyone have known about Jesus? It wasn't on the front page of the newspapers because there were no newspapers then and Bethlehem wasn't on the internet at that time! So the angels were the most important part, and you'll be a sweet angel. You just need a pair of wings and you'll be all set."

Frances looked Rover in the eye and said, "I don't need wings because I'm not an angel. The farm geese are the angels. They are beautiful and they already have wings. Usually some Canada geese want to be angels too. They have strong voices and fly all over the place so they would do a great job of spreading good news".

Rover nodded in agreement and said, "Well, I am still having a hard time figuring out your part in the play. I know! You must be one of the wise ones! They came from far-off lands. In their wisdom, they marvelled at the beauty of nature, especially the stars in the night sky. They observed a new star one night and they knew it meant that someone very special had been born. They followed the star to Bethlehem and brought gifts of gold, frankincense and myrrh. After their visit they went back to their faraway places to tell others about a baby that would bring love to the world. They were important, so you must be a wise man. "

"Nope," replied the little lamb, "they are very cool but I'm not a wise man. There are three owls that are the wise ones. To be honest they kind of give me the creeps. They come swooping in from the east with little pretend gifts in their sharp talons. But I guess it is better that they have those things in their talons than a wee lamb or one of my small furry friends."

"I see what you mean, Frances," said Rover "but what part do you play? There's not many characters left in the Christmas story. Oh, I've got it! You must be a shepherd. They were in the fields taking care of sheep and little lambs like you. They went to see the new baby too. Maybe they wanted to make sure the baby was safe, just like they kept their flocks safe. They were truly important!"

"No," said Frances, "I'm not a shepherd. We have Amber, a little border collie dog, who likes to be the shepherd and she does a great job of it."

At that point Rover was really wondering who Frances, the little lamb, could be in the Christmas play. To every guess he made, the answer was "no": an ox, a camel, a donkey, a lamb? Always no. When Rover guessed a lamb Frances replied, "Well, you know I'm a lamb, but, really, a lamb is not the most important part of the Christmas story, so that's not what I am in the pageant."

"OK," moaned Rover, "I give up. What part do you have? What is the most important part in the Christmas story?"

"I," began Frances, with great seriousness, "am the manger!"

"The manger?!" exclaimed Rover, his ears going up in that quizzical doggy fashion.

"Yes," stated Frances, with utmost dignity, "I have the most important part. I am the manger!"

Rover was still trying to understand this as he said, "The manger? You mean that sort of box thing from which the animals eat their hay? The thing Mary used as a bed for baby Jesus?"

"Yes," replied Frances excitedly, "that's me!"

Rover looked a little confused. "What's so important about that? I mean Mary could have just held Jesus while he slept."

The little lamb responded with "Yup. She sure could have. But she didn't. She could have held him very close and kept her eyes on him and never let him out of her sight. She could have kept him just for Joseph and herself. He would have simply been their little boy. She could have held onto him all right, but she didn't. She laid him in a manger! Laid him in a manger to share with everyone!"

A light seemed to come into Rover's eyes. "Well, I never thought of it that way before. The manger is so very important!"

Frances was happy that Rover finally understood what she had been trying to tell him. "It is important because I, the manger, am the one to receive the gift of baby Jesus, who is really the gift of love. We can't give love unless we have received it, so the manger, that's me, teaches us that we should accept love and be filled with love, so that we can give it to others."

"Well, Frances, you are a clever little lamb. Thanks for explaining all that to me and telling me about the farmyard Christmas pageant. You have some great critters playing all the parts but I think there is one piece of the puzzle that is missing. Do you have a baby Jesus to lay in the manger?"

"Oh, yes. I lie on my back with all my little hoofs up in the air so I sort of look like a manger. Then my little mouse friend is laid in the manger." said Frances with great tenderness.

Rover exclaimed, "Baby Jesus is a mouse?!"

"Yeah," replied Frances, "because mice are kind of like Jesus; like love. They are everywhere and sometimes even when you can't see them or hear them, they're still there. And besides, this mouse is special. His name is Chris. Chris Mouse. Get it? *Chrismouse*. Kind of like *Christmas*, don't you think? And you know what? Chris really is the most important character and I have the most important part. We make a great team: the one who gives love, who IS love, and the one who receives love. Once love is accepted, it can be given to another who will take it and give it to someone else. They can pass it on to still others, so it keeps being shared over and over again. Before you know it love is everywhere! That is what Christmas is all about."

"Well, that is so true, Frances! I hope you have a lovely time with the farmyard pageant. Merry Christmas!" said Rover.

"Merry Christmas to you too." called Frances as she scampered off happily into the meadow.

The End.

THE AUTHOR

Donna Hert lives on beautiful Vancouver Island, Canada with her wonderful husband of over 40 years. She enjoys the great outdoors and playing violin. She takes delight in her four lovely children, the amazing spouses they chose and the terrific grandchildren they produced!

"For all the beloved ones in my life who have received and shared love so well." - D.H.

THE ILLUSTRATOR

Carolina Vazquez has always enjoyed drawing, but she began getting most involved in it at age nine. She will often use pages from comic books as her inspiration. Besides drawing, Carolina also enjoys going for runs, playing the violin and piano, and doing Irish dance. She has been homeschooled her whole life, and is now in seventh grade. Most importantly, she was taught about how Jesus came to earth to give us eternal life through salvation. She lives on Vancouver Island in British Columbia, Canada.

"To mom" - C.V.